Put Beginning Readers on the Right Track with
ALL ABOARD READING™

The All Aboard Reading series is especially designed for beginning readers. Written by noted authors and illustrated in full color, these are books that children really want to read—books to excite their imagination, expand their interests, make them laugh, and support their feelings. With fiction and nonfiction stories that are high interest and curriculum-related, All Aboard Reading books offer something for every young reader. And with four different reading levels, the All Aboard Reading series lets you choose which books are most appropriate for your children and their growing abilities.

Picture Readers

Picture Readers have super-simple texts, with many nouns appearing as rebus pictures. At the end of each book are 24 flash cards—on one side is a rebus picture; on the other side is the written-out word.

Station Stop 1

Station Stop 1 books are best for children who have just begun to read. Simple words and big type make these early reading experiences more comfortable. Picture clues help children to figure out the words on the page. Lots of repetition throughout the text helps children to predict the next word or phrase—an essential step in developing word recognition.

Station Stop 2

Station Stop 2 books are written specifically for children who are reading with help. Short sentences make it easier for early readers to understand what they are reading. Simple plots and simple dialogue help children with reading comprehension.

Station Stop 3

Station Stop 3 books are perfect for children who are reading alone. With longer text and harder words, these books appeal to children who have mastered basic reading skills. More complex stories captivate children who are ready for more challenging books.

In addition to All Aboard Reading books, look for All Aboard Math Readers™ (fiction stories that teach math concepts children are learning in school) and All Aboard Science Readers™ (nonfiction books that explore the most fascinating science topics in age-appropriate language).

All Aboard for happy reading!

For Mom and Dad—E.B.N.

In memory of Katelyn Webb.
We will forever cherish that special closeness,
and the cuddles shared while reading books
together—Love, Mom & Dad

Text copyright © 2000 by Emily Neye. Illustrations copyright © 2000 by Ron Broda. All rights reserved. Published by Grosset & Dunlap, a division of Penguin Putnam Books for Young Readers, 345 Hudson Street, New York, NY 10014. GROSSET & DUNLAP and ALL ABOARD SCIENCE READER are trademarks of Penguin Putnam Inc. Published simultaneously in Canada. Printed in the U.S.A.

Library of Congress Cataloging-in-Publication Data

Neye, Emily
    Butterflies / by Emily Neye ; illustrated by Ron Broda.
        p. cm. — (All aboard reading. Level 1)
    Summary: Describes the appearance, life cycle, habits, habitat, and winter migration
of butterflies.
    1. Butterflies—Juvenile literature. [1.Butterflies.] I. Broda, Ron, ill. II. Title. III. Series.
    QL 544.2 .N49 2000
    595.78'9—dc21   00-025925

ISBN 0-448-42280-8 (GB)   A B C D E F G H I J

ISBN 0-448-41966-1 (pbk.)   D E F G H I J

Butterflies

By Emily Neye
Illustrated by Ron Broda

Grosset & Dunlap • New York

Butterflies live
all over the world.
They are in backyard gardens.

They are in

rainforests far away.

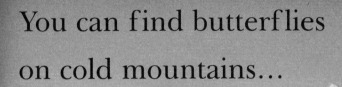

You can find butterflies on cold mountains...

and in hot deserts.

Butterflies are insects
like flies and ladybugs.
They have six legs,
a body in three parts,
and skin that is hard like a shell.
Like most insects,
butterflies have wings.

There are more than
twenty thousand kinds
of butterflies.
They come in
all different colors.

Butterflies come
in different sizes.
The biggest butterfly has wings
as wide as a robin's wings.

The smallest butterfly
is about the size
of this picture.

But every butterfly
starts out the same way—
as a tiny egg.

This monarch butterfly
(you say it like this: MON-ark)
has just laid
one of her eggs on a leaf.

egg

A few days later,
the egg hatches.
Now it is a tiny caterpillar.

All the caterpillar does is
eat and rest,
eat and rest.
It chews up many leaves.
It grows and grows.

Two weeks go by.
Now the caterpillar
is ready to change.
It finds a safe spot
on a twig or leaf.
It spins a silk pad.
It hangs down from the pad.

It looks as if
the caterpillar is just resting.
But it isn't!
Slowly, it sheds its skin.
Then it forms a hard shell.
Inside the shell,
the caterpillar is changing.

After about a week,
the shell cracks open.
Out comes a pretty
monarch butterfly!

Her wings are wet.
She can't fly yet.
She must let her wings
dry in the sun.

Then the monarch flies
to a bed of flowers.
She is hungry.

Butterflies do not eat leaves
like caterpillars.
They suck sweet juices
from flowers.
Their tongues work like straws.

Some animals like
to eat butterflies.
But these butterflies are safe.
Their wings look like
leaves and bark.
This bird does not see them.
Can you see them?

Are these butterflies?

No. They are moths.

Moths look a lot like butterflies.

But they fly at night.

Butterflies fly in the daytime.

Is this a butterfly?
Yes!
You can tell
because its wings
are closed.

When a moth rests,
its wings stay open.

The summer is ending.
Fall is on the way.

Most butterflies do not
like the cold.
Some sleep all winter.
They find quiet spots,
such as a cave or your attic.

Other butterflies fly south
to warm places.

Monarch butterflies
fly many, many miles.
Clouds of them fill the sky.
In the spring,
they fly back north.
There, they will lay
their eggs.

And soon,
new butterflies will be here.
Maybe some will be
in your backyard!